BITISM

CRYPTIC

ANARCHY

Leon Tusk

iUniverse books may be ordered through booksellers or by contacting:

iUniverse
1663 Liberty Drive
Bloomington, IN 47403
www.iuniverse.com
844-349-9409

Because of the dynamic nature of the Internet, any web addresses or links contained in this book may have changed since publication and may no longer be valid. The views expressed in this work are solely those of the author and do not necessarily reflect the views of the publisher, and the publisher hereby disclaims any responsibility for them.

Any people depicted in stock imagery provided by Getty Images are models, and such images are being used for illustrative purposes only.
Certain stock imagery © Getty Images.

ISBN: 978-1-6632-4448-2 (sc)
ISBN: 978-1-6632-4452-9 (hc)
ISBN: 978-1-6632-4451-2 (e)

Library of Congress Control Number: 2022915650

Print information available on the last page.

iUniverse rev. date: 10/06/2022

BITISM

Bitism is the practice of Counter-economics with the means to remove third-party verification, thus removing institutional regulatory systems. Bitism supports the direct action in the decentralization of economic monetization by using blockchain technology, also known as Web3. Bitists are free-market enthusiasts, based on society's mutual willingness to participate. Bitists share a common philosophy of economic transparency and individual property; and through the means of cryptography, value individual privacy and freedom. The anarcho-bitist advocates for chaos through action in regard to the transition to decentralized machine monetization, or Web3. The anarcho-bitist exploits every advantage cryptocurrencies have to offer to their individual freedom. Only through one's expansion of ideas, knowledge, and action, can the Bitist achieve liberation for themselves and for others from crony institutions and economic enslavement. Bitists are critical of institutions, Bitcoin Maximalist, and Marxist theory. Bitism's main influences are Samuel Edward Konkin III, Max Stirner, Diogenes, Agorism, Egoism, and Stoicism.

This book is dedicated to Samuel Edward Konkin III, Max Stirner, Diogenes, and one Anonymous friend. I only hope this adds another limb to the tree of anarchy, as it becomes very apparent that it goes thirsty. Samuel Edwards Konkin III thoughts on Counter-economics were the main drive and inspiration for this book. Agorism is what got us this far and unfortunately it is time we talk about it. It's obvious we are selling out the free-market for individual wealth. I wanted to bring an old philosopher back to life as well. Max Stirner warned us all about interference from the state, and after two centuries I think it is time to have an honest discussion about ourselves and legislative freedoms. Max Stirner understood individual ownership and individual value from the state better than anyone. Finally, he who should not be named, Diogenes. What strange coincidence we get to enjoy Diogenes and Dogecoin. I know if Diogenes was here today, he would just call us all, *"try hards"*.

"The more we try to define and understand Bitcoin, we take away its uniqueness, thus taking away its freedom." My thoughts after the Cryptocurrency Congressional Hearing Dec 9, 2021

BITCOIN FOR THE SMOOTH BRAIN

First, understand that this is merely my interpretation of what Bitcoin and cryptocurrencies are. Diogenes lives in all of us, so I say, to the Bitcoin intellectual, "In 100 years, when they dig up your bones, they won't know if you were holding Bitcoin or Dogecoin". I was far too lazy to read a book on the subject, yet somehow still moved by it. It could possibly be because the word *"freedom"* keeps getting tossed around, and it has grabbed my attention. Everything I understand or misunderstand about economics is through casual reading and lectures from economists. I'm not trying to sell you anything about myself or my personal beliefs and values. I have both red days and green days. I would like for you to draw your own conclusions and create your own ideas.

It seems as though Bitcoin and cryptocurrency enthusiasts are desperate for a philosophical view. Some of you have tumbled down the rabbit hole to nowhere and this book is the *"Inception"* to cryptocurrency. The rabbit hole to your soul is more valuable than someone's idea. Those of us that understand the rabbit hole already know the rabbit just ends up staring at its own arse. A bunny rabbit ouroboros is definitely in order, seeing how the rabbit hole operates more like a wormhole. This book is as close as Bitcoin will ever get to solving the space-time problem.

Also, it appears as though gold barons, environmentalists, governments, and Bitcoin Maximalists all want a war with cryptocurrency. Let's give them one! The idea in which anyone expects a common person to understand the complexity of what Bitcoin is, is a shot to the moon. The saying goes, "A fool and his money are soon parted." Personally, I believe it is as simple or as complicated as you want it to be. To me, it's nothing but another clam shell. However, let us not forget we have a female Supreme Court judge that can't define what a woman is. My lack of confidence in our institution's ability to understand or even define Bitcoin weighs heavy. So I'll do my best, in *layman's terms.* We'll get to institutional incompetency later on in the book.

Bitcoin is digital money meant for peer to peer transactions. The data is stored on a decentralized ledger, known as a blockchain. The transaction is verified through a system of validators, better known as "bitcoin miners", thus eliminating the need for third-party verification, i.e. regulatory institutions. Every individual has his or her own cryptocurrency wallet. Individuals make peer to peer transactions with what is referred to as a "hot wallet". A hot wallet is always connected to the internet, thus allowing validators to process transactions. Cold wallets, or "cold storage", is a cryptocurrency wallet off-line and less-vulnerable to cyber attacks. Cold storage is primarily used for investors looking for future gains.

Yawn... Now, what the hell did I just say?!

It's ok, I am going to break it down, Barney style. Remember that purple dinosaur who taught the children their 1,2,3's and A,B,C's? That Barney.

Now, I want to start off with a question for you: Did everyone freak the hell out in the past about debit cards? I'm just asking, because explaining machine science and economic theory isn't exactly the easiest subject. Do they actually know how their debit card works or did everyone just start using it blindly? Everyone's got to over-complicate it, I guess.

Before we can understand digital currency, we must first understand "currencies", in general. We all know we started out with the bartering system. "I'll give you five bananas if you give me three Taco Bell supreme crunch wraps." Good thing we got away from that system of trade! And then, in steps currencies. First, it was shells, then precious metals, and finally, notes or dollars. Everything and everyone that assigned these forms of currencies and their values were of a higher class; they probably had a lot of it, so they convinced people it was worth something and thus, giving them control over people. The dollar is merely held up by faith. This is no different with Bitcoin. However, institutions set the dollar's value, unlike Bitcoin. Does this mean Bitcoin holds no value? No. Bitcoin's value is on display for everyone to see. And the faith is in the technology. The standard dollar holds value in the institution's eyes because banks can create debt with loans. Also, governments create higher and/ or newer taxes for profit. This is the reason why we are all told to have faith in the dollar; it merely serves *their* purpose.

"Wait a minute! Didn't we just pay crypto taxes?!" -Why, yes. Yes, we did. This confirms the government has recognized its value.

"Well aren't the banks giving out loans?!" -Also, yes. Goldman Sachs offered its first-ever lending facility that is backed by Bitcoin. This confirms, now, that the banking industry recognizes its value. What you do with it, or for it, is how you choose to value it. The major difference is not one man, one institution, or one country that has their hand on Bitcoin's pulse. It is transparent in its value for everyone, not just institutions. Your current dollar is in a constant state of fluctuation in value as well. You just don't see it until the system crashes. If your money is transparent, you can better prepare yourself for whatever the current God King decides to do with the money printer. It's just another clam shell, boys.

Current transactions are settled all because the third-party, i.e. the state, sets the current value of the note. This means peer-to-peer transactions with cash, we just agree that a dollar is dollar because we've been told that it is. A transaction with a debit card works the same way, but transactions are sent through the magical internet in the sky and verified through centralized servers, where a ledger is then stored. It is also machine monetization, but there is a huge difference when using Bitcoin. Only special authorities are allowed to see this ledger, and they have the ability to see every transaction without anyone knowing. They can also track anyone at will, without any regard to our 4th amendment rights. Because of these servers being centralized, they are more vulnerable to cyber attacks. Eventually, all financial services will be moved to blockchain technology due to the iron-clad security features. Now you understand the basics of how your debit card works. *Neat.*

Are you still awake??

Essentially, Bitcoin transactions work the same as your debit card, but with a lot of key differences. The first major difference is how the transactions are verified. Transactions must travel through several blocks within the blockchain, and each block must verify its authenticity. If a block is to ever come under attack, it just notifies the other blocks, thus canceling the entire transaction. This is also why Bitcoin has never been hacked. All the blocks are competing for verification and rewarding the blocks with Bitcoin. This is why people mine Bitcoin. Bitcoin's ledger is stored on a decentralized blockchain and can be seen by everyone, not just some special authority figures. The difference is that we have constant transparency in all transactions, yet they remain anonymous; hidden behind a long line of code, reinstating your 4th amendment rights. Personally, I just imagine a network of calculators competing to solve the same math problem.

Do you trust your calculator more than your government?

Now, let's talk about wallets. Remember when I just said "you remain anonymous; hidden behind a long line of code." That code is your individual wallet address. We wouldn't be very good at sending e-mails to one another without an email address. The same concept goes for cryptocurrencies. So, if we are having to compare peer-to-peer transactions to sending your buddy an e-mail as the best way to explain it, then so be it.

What is more important about cryptowallets is distinguishing between what's referred to "hot" and "cold" wallets. I already gave a brief explanation, but let's go a little more in-depth. If you're using a cold wallet, you bought Bitcoin from an exchange and it was then moved to a cold wallet or cold storage. They have also been referred to as "hard wallets". It's absolutely safe. Even if the Feds come knocking, you just lost that cold wallet in a "boating accident." *Wink.* The 2nd Amendment enthusiast will get what I'm saying. The only time your Bitcoin is in danger is when it's stored in a hot wallet, because it's technically not your keys. It's the exchange holding the Bitcoin on your hot wallet.

"WassaWassaWassup! Bitconnect"!

Everyone needs to Google "Bitconnect" before you choose an exchange. Personally, I tend to go with FTX, and it is honestly for one ridiculous reason; Sam Bankman Fried, CEO of FTX went out and got the G.O.A.T. If Tom Brady, the Golden Boy goes down in flames, then it's clear we never had a chance.

"We "conserve" nothing; neither do we want to return to any past periods; we are not by any means "liberal"; we do not work for "progress"; we do not need to plug up our ears against the sirens who in the marketplace sing of the future: their song about "equal rights," "a free society," "no more masters and no servants" has no allure for us". - Friedrich Nietzsche

DCA AND PLAY THE LEVELS

Investopedia defines Dollar-Cost Averaging, or DCA, as an investment strategy in which an investor divides up the total amount of said investment to be invested across periodic purchases of a target asset in an effort to reduce the impact of volatility on the overall purchase. The purchases occur regardless of the asset's price and at regular intervals. In effect, this strategy removes much of the detailed work of attempting to time the market in order to make purchases of equities at the best prices. Dollar-cost averaging is also known as the Constant Dollar Plan.

I don't how you feel, but I think that's playing a little too loose with my assets. No doubt, it's a great strategy if you're looking for long-term gains and you're holding enough fiat currency to bleed out all over the market, "catching knives" or red candles. What I mean by that, is if you forget to zoom out and watch the yearly accumulation levels, you can get caught buying a dip... within a dip, within a dip. It remains a great strategy, simply, because Bitcoin is inevitable due to its supply. It is also a very simple practice. The easiest practice of which is investing in weekly buys, no matter Bitcoin's current price. Just get ready to buckle up and HODL *(hold on for dear life)!*

Now, when and where I make my periodic purchases defines the term "playing the levels." To determine what the levels are is what we refer to as accumulation, or support and resistance levels. This is how I apply my own DCA strategy. I will be using $200 to demonstrate. Obviously you can apply some simple math to fit your current value. First, I'm going to divide my currency into percentages. In this case using $200, I'm going to maintain 20% ($40) in whatever fiat currency I'm using.

Next I'll divide the rest into purchases of 10% ($20), 15% ($30), 25% ($50), and 30% ($60) of the same fiat currency. My reasoning behind this is to feel less pain. We could have just divided the $200 into equal, quartered increments of $50. Sure that's a much simpler DCA strategy, until you put $50 on a level that is 10% from its all time high.

Remember, you have to maintain the mindset, "what goes up will come down." Bitcoin is like a bouncy ball going up a ramp. No matter how much the institutions pump it making the ball bounce higher, gravity is going happen, thus creating a dip. When you decided to put $50 (25% of your entire value and also 10% from Bitcoin's all-time high), I put 10%, or only $20. That way, in case gravity is to occur, I'm in a much less damaging financial position than the person using a simpler DCA strategy. I'm also holding more fiat currency to buy back in.

You might be asking yourself, "But what about the 20% ($40) you did nothing with?" Well, boys, this couldn't possibly go tits up, right?? That last 20% is for if/when Bitcoin does some crazy dip, breaking all support levels. I'm a firm believer, not a cultist. I will demonstrate my DCA using five buy areas with a current five-year chart and some "garage math". Garage math is math that's just… *close enough.* The point of this chart is to keep it as simple as possible. You'll be responsible for finding accumulation levels in the future. In fact, you're responsible for everything as this is not financial advice. You can YOLO *(you only live once)* your life savings into PooCoin, for all I care.

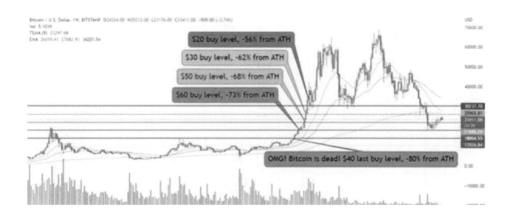

With all that having been said, you might be left in a state of bewilderment. "How the hell is money going to work like this?" you might be asking.

Listen carefully. This is how a free-market operates. You're going to have good days and you're going to be eating ramen noodles on other days. I ate a lot of spaghetti growing up as a kid and that hasn't changed. I just eat a hell of a lot more steak nowadays, as well. When the scales begin to balance, people lose while others win. But if it stays free, it will always naturally tip back and forth. You buy Bitcoin at the price you deserve to own Bitcoin. No asset, country, or external value should ever be placed over you. People have jumped from buildings losing everything they valued. Value yourself over Bitcoin. It's only money; just another clam shell.

Really, the best advice is just to buy a little Bitcoin and make stupid bets with friends or pay back IOU's in Bitcoin. Just play with it first, then ask yourself if you're ready to take a ride on the freedom rocket. Can you handle the volatility of its nature? If not, get out now. It's not for the weak individuals that are always seeking Big Brothers helping hand. They'll mess it up for the rest of us. Peace out commie.

"Buy the dip, fa***t." -Warren Buffett *(probably)*

COMPUTING SCIENCE VS. POTATO

The Micheal Saylor vs. Frank Giustra/ Bitcoin vs. Gold debate, debating which one is better, was mostly argued in terms of institutional value. Individual value is situational value and cannot be felt or understood by either party in regard to your freedom. Frank Giustra describes Bitcoin as volatile while praising gold's value based solely on people's willingness to kill, steal, and go to war to obtain it. Gold has only proven man's volatility. It is a poison to our humanity. Gold has failed several times in the last two centuries and is no longer used for monetary accountability. History already decided gold's outcome. I'll never get back those two hours of listening to a man explain to me what a lump of metal is. *Yawn.*

We're starting to get into the good stuff. I wasn't going to bore you with just another lame book about cryptocurrency. Let's riot!

Frank's main argument boils down to simply this: Are you currently happy with the status quo? Do you want to continue to trust the institutions to make life choices on your behalf? Spare us your roads paved of gold, we see the blood that washes it shiny! Your metal of malice dulls with tongues! Frank, in one instance during the debate, referred to Bitcoin as "anarchy". *Mmmmmm, yes more.* So, the two hour, mind-numbing discussion of "Which is better, computing science or a potato?" wasn't a total waste. In other words, I got my dopamine hit. Shame the Egoist!

How gold is manipulated versus how Bitcoin is manipulated varies. You can inflate gold, copy it, and confiscate it. A Bitist doesn't trouble himself with the same insecurities as the gold investor, though, simply because of transparency and cryptic security. *Up only.* As for the Bitcoin investor, he doesn't have to rely on institutional value. This creates decentralized transparent value, or pure democratic value. 1 Bitcoin = 1 Bitcoin. The Bitcoin investor only has to ask themselves one question: "Is the dollar always losing value?"

Frank believes Bitcoin is a threat to the US dollar. On the contrary, the institutions that devalued the dollar is the threat. These are the very institutions that he is convincing gold buyers to have trust in. A dollar backed by Bitcoin is infinite and transparent.

All governmental currencies now have that ability. The more transparent the global currency becomes, the more foreign governments can trust one another, thus creating better trade. And I say this with a very nihilistic tone, *ending global conflicts.*

The misconception of Bitcoin being a threat to the US dollar is absolutely wrong. Institutional failure, which led to the 2008 housing market crash, was the final threat to the US dollar. Bitcoin was created in 2009. What a weird coincidence, right? Yes, we all understand we printed trillions of dollars, therefore, devaluing the dollar. What really happened is the beginning of an economic war with the world. You will hear a lot of rhetoric about China's economic war with the US, but what does it all mean? Is it due to trade?

It is very simple to understand if you import more than you export. You'll just create more debt. China figured out real quick that the U.S. wasn't going to pay their debts. China's currency is backed by the U.S. dollar due to it being the current global currency of trade. China felt the effects of all the money being printed and, in return, began buying up all market assets. To counter China and the rest of the world's run on the markets, our institutions, with all their wisdom, started buying all market assets as well. This is why we are looking at an over-inflated market from all aspects of said assets. This is why you can't buy a house these days. Still don't believe me? The total housing market capitalization in 2010 was roughly 21 trillion dollars. Today it stands at 43 trillion dollars. How many people own a home has little to do with the housing market capitalization. I'm only pointing out that food, water, and shelter (homes) are human life's necessities and it is being measured by crony institutions.

Who killed the American dream, though?

In all fairness, the American dream was created by the institutions to sell you debt. However, it was at least beneficial to both parties. The institutions walked away with billions of dollars and the individual homeowner walked away with an asset.

Who kills all ideas? And how will your current institutions sell you a future?

Sure, I'm just a big conspiratorialist. I am more than confident that "shadow banks" and other institutions will be transparent in their operations. Why sell us into debt when we can just be born into it? By that I mean, they just buy all the homes and crank up the rent. I've heard a lot of rhetoric about how Millennials and Gen Z "prefer to rent" instead of owning a home. Wow, really?! That's what the venture capitalists and various institutions want to convince everyone into believing?!

Here's an idea: fight me. If the venture capitalist and their crony institutions truly believe in something so blatantly false and want to stand for it, then they should pick a McDonald's parking lot and pull up. They are all ruthless con-artists peddling a false narrative, and nothing more. Like most things, this is simply "cause and effect" that will only lead to more socialist ideas. If the capitalist wishes to survive, they can buy digital assets that require zero maintenance fees and use hard wallets to avoid taxes. But who am I to tell another man how to spend his money?!

To get back to the point of "Computing Science Vs. Potato", Frank believes institutions will not give up their gold or transition willingly... and he's right. They hold all the gold and all the power, thus controlling your life. Where is he wrong? He believes that they have a choice. With mass adoption and the public's willingness to use Bitcoin, the institutions will have no choice but to buy and honor its value in order to maintain their relevance. In other words, they will pull the rug out from under themselves if they are not careful. Gold has failed many times over the years and was simply revived because a secret group of individuals that you never met, nor elected, just changed its monetary value. They actually did it so many times it destabilized world trade, which led to even more conflicts. This is why we are no longer held to the gold standard. I bet Frank almost had a heart attack when Uganda uncovered twelve trillion dollars worth of mineable gold. In theory, this should have sent the gold market crashing but thanks to state regulation- I mean communism, it did not.

We'll just ignore it.

In essence, Bitcoin is decentralized monetary democracy. All democracy sounds good from the start. Did Satoshi Nakamoto get it right this time? Were individual human ambitions standing in the way of democracy? That's hard to believe, right?!

Micheal Saylor truly speaks the Bitcoin gospel. His philosophy is unique and can be verified through historic fact. Micheal sees and understands money for what it really is: Energy... It has the power to move people and disrupt current systems. In order to be free of institutional monetary systems you must first own your value. Many Bitcoin Maximalists and myself all understand that our individual value is more important than our institutional value. Micheal is looking at Bitcoin through the eyes of institutions and its importance to global trade and maintaining transparency for governments to coexist. The Bitist is left in the middle, understanding both sides. If Micheal wants to push Bitcoin into mass global adaptation, we are definitely here to support. With that having been said, if they want to mess it up and tax us to death, the Bitist will move on to a different cryptocurrency maintaining their individual ideology. Basically, I'm saying that we are going to keep creating magical internet money, and they can't stop us. We do not care what institutions think or value.

The summation of my final thoughts on the subject is this: If you are reading this book during a bear market, chances are that I am confirming your ego's conspiratorial thoughts. If you are reading this during a bull market, I probably look like just another stupid science bitch, confirming situational value is, indeed, pure value. I digress.

"No man knows the value of innocence and integrity, but he who has lost them." -William Godwin

BITISM VS. THE "GREENIE MEANIES"

Today's coins are made from metals such as nickel, copper, and zinc. Gold and other metals are considered stores of value. All these "precious metals" are mined buy slave labor (mainly consisting of children) in the poorest of countries. What do you think all this human trafficking is for? Sure, Jeffery Epstein, who totally "killed himself," probably had a few sex slaves. But the largest influence for human trafficking is slave labor. Is this good for the environment? Have you seen the pictures of surrounding environments of mining facilities? An individual slave might just think their current environment or climate is less than satisfying. Imagine that! Sometimes, when I'm in deep thought, I try my best to understand and be empathetic to their situations.

Obviously, I fall short because it's scientifically impossible to literally feel someone else's feelings. This is the absolute reason I know that the environmentalists are only serving their collective ego and not the world's collective values, if there even is such a thing. There is no such thing as global value in my eyes. It is simply the "greater good," which sounds a lot like the basis of a cult. Like most cults, if you are not at the top then you run the chance of being sacrificed. We can't just value being alive. That's just silly. We value what we do while we're alive. I'm not going to lie, this part of the book is my favorite and absolutely satisfies my egoist thirst.

Riot like a sir...

Environmentalists care without any thought or solutions. They fall under the Non-player Character, or "NPC," definition; a meme that cuts through the heart of humanity. The urban dictionary explains a NPC as; An NPC is seemingly a human that is unable to think objectively. We exist in a simulated reality and some humans take on the role of NPCs, spouting "opinions" they are programmed to claim and regurgitate in a cult-like manner.

Every single time an institution fails someone's individual values, the internet ignites with the dumbest of collective activist ideas and individual statements. The NPC is an institutional activist bot. It's a clown world and they all honk. The anarchist and an individual free-thinker is always left holding the popcorn. It is much like watching a self-imposed mental clinic.

The environmentalist, with infinite wisdom and a scientific brain, somehow elected Greta Thunberg as the CEO of the proverbial "psych ward" and Alexandria Ocasio-Cortez (AOC) as its Director of Operations. I am not going to insult Greta. In fact, I have some empathy because her uniqueness was taken from her at such an early age. She will never be anything more than a misguided, institutionalized activist and I find that sad. I guess I should feel that way about all the young children activists. The culture war is real, but it is under a false pretext. They're stealing your children's freedom of thought by shaming independent thinkers into conforming to collective whims, leaving them open and vulnerable for exploitation.

AOC, on the other hand is a grown woman hiding behind institutional feminism and a bullshit Arts and Science degree. Could a college degree be any more veg than "Arts and Science Degree". It is meant to be a stepping stone to further your education, thus gaining a degree that holds merit. "Arts and Science degrees" might as well fall under whatever category that gives out participation ribbons. AOC is ridiculous and hides under the guise of being a political intellectual, as well as a sympathizer. She is just another clown at the loony bin and the typical conformist drinks her kool-aid. She never deserved the spotlight, but I'm really glad she got it. My cynical dark humor gets tickled every time she speaks. Don't worry, Representative Ted Yoho, I got this. Now, before she stands in front of congress for ten minutes wasting everyone's time and taxpayer money whining about how I am calling her bad names and, therefore, accusing me of being a sexist racist, or a white national extremist, Al Gore is a cunt. How's that for an *"Inconvenient Truth"*, Al?! Everyone slow clap for AOC: The institutional feminist.

So powerful, so brave, much wow.

Now back to the business at hand. To quote Theodore Roosevelt, "Complaining about a problem without posing a solution is called 'whining'." Bitcoin globally consumes 150 terawatt hours of electricity, annually. In the United States, nuclear plants produce 778 terawatt hours, *"thanks Google".* See the solution yet? Not only are we solving environmentalist carbon solutions with clean energy, but we're freeing the poorest of countries of economic enslavement. Does the environmentalist care at all about humanity itself?! Isn't the argument based around how well the ecosystem will be left for future generations? What about now?! I need to calm down; I apologize. If you spend enough time in the greenie meanie psych ward, you tend to lose your mind. There is truly no way of trying to rationalize the way these people think. Even though I more or less offered the best and most logical solution to Bitcoin's energy consumption by creating nuclear facilities in industrialized countries, thus creating valuable jobs. Nope!! Here comes the damn environmentalist with their damn solar energy bullshit! Ahhhh!! I'm never going to escape the greenie meanie psych ward!

Almighty Diogenes, grant me your strength!

Solar energy enthusiasts miss the point as well. There is no such thing as clean if it is produced through slave labor, whether that be through means of slave wages or forced labor camps. Communist China just so happens to be the main exporter of solar energy, and they have both. I mean honestly what's the plan here? Just turn our eyes away from all the horrifying atrocities the Communist party commits? Does the environmentalist honestly not understand how valuable the jobs are we create by producing our own energy? What happens to the countries buying energy instead of selling it? Who is welcome in their new Garden of Eden? Are you worthy of your master's desire? Who will tend to their new Garden of Eden? Is it work your master desires? Everyone slow clap for the solar energy enthusiast that disregards his fellow man for a "better future". *Yawn.*

You must understand, this is in no way directed at the Bitcoin miners using solar energy. Through my eyes, you are the guards of the psych ward and you're doing your best. The lesser of two evils is not really my thing, but it's their misguided beliefs slowing us down. El Salvador is an even better example to solving Bitcoin's, as well as the world's, energy consumption. Using geothermal energy, which is naturally created from volcanoes, essentially works the same way as a nuclear power plant operates, but without the radioactive materials. There are one hundred and sixty-nine *(nice)* volcanoes in the United States of America, alone. The individual anarchist is probably thinking, "what the hell, bro?! What's with all this collective thinking?"

First of all, I can dig up radioactive material, buy a swimming-pool at Walmart, throw some rebar into the ground, pour some concrete over it, slap a turbine on top, hook it to a generator, and create my own current. The problem lies within my damn government not allowing me! I understand why the community might be concerned. Fair enough, though. I wouldn't exactly trust myself to operate a nuclear power plant, either.

Much science, very wow.

This is my way of trying to save a few dodo birds from falling off the cliff while they are following mindlessly behind Bernie Sanders, Alexandria Ocasio-Cortez, Elizabeth Warren, and Richard Wolff. If you want to throw them from a helicopter afterwards, who am I to stop another man from his freedom? That's a joke for the ANCAP. *Wink.*

I was once required to get a license through the United States Environmental Protection Agency, or EPA, for a Maintenance Technician position. Anyone that has ever been required to take the courses and pass the test, understands chlorine molecules are the greatest threat to the ozone layer and global climate change. The Obama administration went through great lengths in regard to how we handle these chemicals. I am not upset about the regulations; I only found them pointless because China and India didn't implement any regulations. Where are all the activists screaming about global chlorine admissions? We literally have a holiday dedicated to planting trees that help eliminate CO_2 gasses. Maybe they should research, "Great Green Wall".

"So plant a tree, hippie!"

Party of science, my arse!! I never even got vaccinated for COVID-19 and its various mutations because we have over two centuries of data on how vaccines are produced and work. The scientists that discovered these vaccines were awarded the Nobel Peace Prize when the award still held merit. Sure, let's get our health advice from watching Steven Colbert dancing around like a monkey while spurting one-sided propaganda. For shame the Egoist!

Before any environmentalist tries to remind me how the minerals in our machines are dug out of the ground or produced, I will simply say this: We put a dent in the problem. Our machines work, and we do not necessarily need more machines. It is, more so, a means to an end. Also we can use upgrades- the Lightning Network being the best example, yet. The Marxists are all about cracking a few eggs to make an omelet, but they never stop cracking eggs. Their ideas of environmental progress is their moral regress. Their moral unity of slavery drowns with tears from those of greater spirit. It is through will that Sisyphus is able to move his rock. For those without, only have but will to live, spirit is pure and idea becomes pure progress. Amazing how the Marxist environmentalist never said anything about cryptocurrency's energy consumption or about minerals being dug out of the ground until it started changing the financial systems, especially to a decentralized financial system. *Yawn.*

We are truly arriving at my favorite part of my book. I like to think everyone enjoys a good show just so long as they are not in it. We all sit and eat popcorn while people argue online during political debates or good old fashion brawls. It's like watching a dumpster fire and some people really enjoy throwing gas on top of it. Shame the Egoist!

The psych ward is an amusing place to visit, but I would never want to live there.

"I pissed on the man who called me a dog. Why was he so surprised"? -Diogenes

BITISM REKTS INSTITUTIONAL FREEDOM, INSTITUTIONAL VALUE, AND THE CULTURE WAR

The Fraser Institute defines economic freedom as "Individuals having economic freedom when property they acquire without the use of force, fraud, or theft, is protected from physical invasions by others. They are free to use, exchange, or give their property as long as their actions do not violate the identical rights of others."

Well, boys... I hate to break it to you, but this is yet another lie. Economic freedom is simply choice. Identical freedom is collective theory. Using blockchain technology, we have eliminated the need for collective economic theory and have transitioned into a transparent machine monetization.

"Never send a human to do a machine's job." -Agent Smith, The Matrix

You do not ask for economic freedom through institutional legislation, quite simply, because institutions do not understand your individual freedom. You are your own bank; therefore, you are your own value. Buy. Sell. Hold. Hack. Scam. These are the constructs of our situational value that leads to our individual freedoms. No church in the wild, only spirituality! *Yippee-ki-yay!!*

"Congress shall make no law respecting an establishment of religion, or prohibiting the free exercise thereof; or abridging the freedom of speech, or of the press; or the right of the people peaceably to assemble, and to petition the Government for a redress of grievances." -First Amendment to the United States Constitution

It's a trap!

"Bitcoin is text. Bitcoin is speech. It cannot be regulated in a free country like the USA with guaranteed inalienable rights and a First Amendment that explicitly excludes the act of publishing from government oversight." -Beautyon

It's a trap!

Again, this is another misconception of freedom. Max Stirner, when asked about freedom of speech and of the press, Max argued against the idea of legislating human rights. "If I have to ask, then I am not truly free." Max would also argue that, through legislating freedom of the press, it would later become freedom of institutional press. Nearly two hundred years later, we now have CNN, MSNBC, FOX, and massive social media censorship. What do you think the FCC is for?

Another thought on Beautyon's statement is that Bitcoin is text. Sure, I'll give him that the white paper explaining Bitcoin is actual text. However, if I hand it to a common American, it might as well be written in Chinese. Therefore, Bitcoin remains unique. When it is finally applied, it becomes binary; illegible, limitless, and free.

Our government doesn't uphold the constitution, so why hide behind it? Our first amendment rights are getting slowly chipped away. Our second amendment rights are getting chipped away. And our fourth amendment rights are no longer existent. It was written simple enough for everyone to interpret, yet it's no longer functioning. I don't think the constitution is going to help us anymore nor was it ever meant to.

There's no denying the similarities between a Bitist and a Bitcoin Maximalist/constitutionalist. I know a few of you have heard the theory "God Money".

Well if God was a lobster, he would have pinchers...

So let's test the theory. It was Bitcoin that saved Wikileaks and not the constitution. My children, have you lost your way? What have my disciples Julian Assange and Edward Snowden taught you? Is it greed or institutional thinking blinding your path? *Pinch.*

Nothing cracks me up more than listening to a republican talking point comparing capitalism and free-markets. The term capitalism literally came from the state regulating markets. Nothing can make the law just, so the individual and state are at constant odds. In other words, it's all communism boys. The institution's idea of what they tell you a free-market is. Is probably the most blatant misleading lie ever told. Right up there with your constitutional rights.

Nick Land's theory on Accelerationism is reckless and the most dangerous thing I've ever read. The idea to drastically intensify a societal ideology "capitalism" without giving any awareness of the outcome or the current state that it's in can be viewed as juvenile. Mass "social therapy" with one single ideology is incredibly shortsighted and can be proven incorrect with the mass application therapeutics.

Not one drug works the same for everyone!

It's a really easy concept to see how things have gotten better over time. The idea of accelerationism is pretty much the idea of speeding up time in order to gain progress. It took ten years to write the code to get the space shuttle to the moon. How is accelerating an ideology supposed to help with that? Let's not forget about Sputnik, and how close the Space Race actually was.

Nick forgot to take into account that it's all communism, therefore accelerating government. The idea to accelerate capitalism is essentially "global capitalism" which is globalism, which is Marxism. My interpretation is that Nick felt it was in our best interest to sacrifice freedom for a "better future". Imagine sprinkling just a little systemic cybernetics on top of Nick Land's theory and how stupid everyone would become? Let's accelerate people's psychosis because people don't matter right?! QAnon gets it!! *The Skin-walker is real, Mwhahahaha!!* Crank up the volume and rip the knob off!! The only thing Nick Land got right was people were going into the future unwillingly without a choice. No matter if you're dragged into the future kicking and screaming, the illusion was always choice. It appears Nick in the end, got a taste of his own medicine. Thanks, Nick! *Derp.*

I might as well throw a little shade at Jordan Peterson while I'm at it since he seems to have a basic concept of postmodernism. Listening to Jordan Peterson talk about his theories on postmodernism is absolutely gut wrenching. He has only picked a political side because it's profitable. I can't believe after all these years the most intelligent people are still holding onto old corrupted ideologies. I mean in all fairness, this is how the hierarchy was designed after all and what it is meant to do. Jordan Peterson should be thanking Carl Marx for expanding Hegel's ideologies giving Jordan the opportunity to generate as much wealth as possible. He would never have been given the platform to do it, if it wasn't for Marxism. Jordan Peterson is no doubt a great psychologist and should continue his work helping individuals. I actually enjoy listening to Jordan Peterson in some aspects and find him very insightful at times. Jordan just needs to disregard his basic understandings of capitalism and what it means. Jordan wasn't worthy enough to don the fedora. *Aaaarrrgggghhhh! Walk the plank, Peterson!*

I would really enjoy teasing Slavoj Žižek as well. Unfortunately at times it's impossible to understand what "Sylvester" is saying. Philosophy can be very dense at times and trying to comprehend what a cartoon cat is blabbering on about is just exhausting. **Yawn.**

Capitalism and communism are both forms of economic and cultural cuckolding. Here's a postmodern thought: Stop doing the same thing! After saying all that, you can take what you will from it. I'm sure quite a few of you are left puzzled and that's the joys of philosophy. You'll tumble down one rabbit hole to find another and then another.

This book was probably written by the CIA anyways...

The truth about free-markets and capitalism is simply; all free-markets start out free until nature takes course. Newton's Third Law of Motion states "whatever goes up, must come down." Everyone's satisfied when the market is on the up, but when disaster strikes, we go into survival mode. This is when men are either at their weakest or strongest, meaning this is when we are at our most vulnerable. Even a strong man can make an irrational decision during times of chaos. Sometimes they're referred to as heroes, sacrificing their own values for others. A good example is Micheal Saylor buying 1,914 Bitcoins at an average price of $49,229 per Bitcoin. Anyway you want to look at it, that was an expensive grenade he jumped on.

But what if things don't necessarily have to be so disastrous? This is when Big Brother steps in and lends his helping hand. The weaker man, of course, wants the easy way out. The strongest of men, majority of the time, will give into situational value that can be derived from his current environment. In other words, he wants the easy way out, as well. I mean, why run through a brick wall when you can walk around it?

The institutional solution to all problems is simply, "let's just inject more money!"

Things will never get bad, right?

"We can defy the laws of nature, and we'll ride this high forever!"

This is what the federal economist thinks until reality sets in and then the system crashes due to over-inflated currency and global trade stops, because foreign governments and corporations have lost all transparency and trust. The reset button is always the same. The unelected bureaucrats will pick an asset, set a price, and the world moves on. Everyone slow clap for democracy. *Yawn.*

"Those who give up liberty for security deserve neither." - Benjamin Franklin.

Bitcoin is free, and we must endure the hard times to get to the better times that we know are ahead. If we cannot endure the hard times, we'll fail ourselves. Bitcoin runs in cycles so we must plan accordingly. Bitcoin doesn't fail us. I can only speak for myself, though. If I had to choose between decentralized monetary democracy or the current clown show of today, I choose Bitcoin. A Bitist doesn't ask to be free or hide behind the institutional guise of freedom. We are free by choice. We are free because we hold the keys to the locks to our individual value. A guy I know has been pirating movies and software from Pirate Bay for nearly 15 years. Even though the creators were tried and sentenced, Pirate Bay still continues to exist. Good luck finding and arresting Satoshi Nakamoto.

When I was five years old, I swore a pledge to the American flag. When I was twelve years old, I was taught the constitution. When I was twenty-three years old, I swore to uphold an oath to the constitution. Now, I finally understand what it means to be institutionally free. To be quite honest, though, it's not for me. *Semper fi?? Probably not.* Institutional democracy and its freedoms have failed my values. Wave your freedom or set fire, with every meaningless gesture you stifle my desire. It was will that freedom first gestured fire, from fire came ashes, that satisfied desire. Value is situational; It can not be felt nor defined in the halls of institutions. We are not extreme. We are the patrons of the zoo. As I write this, congressional approval sits at 20%, so I know it's failing your value as well. WallstreetBets literally wiped their arse with institutional collective theory on value. They also exposed to everyone how markets are manipulated with the GameStop and AMC squeezes. Can you believe I was kicked out of WallstreetBets for comparing China's social credit scores to capitalist credit scores? Imagine that!

*Side note: I think a guy lost a bet and had to eat a piece of poop. Cheers, apes!

To expose myself for the hypocrite that I am, I still vote to this day. I like to look at it as "weaponized voting." The perfect example of this is voting for Donald Trump. An anarchist could not have possibly asked for a better clown to lead their circus. Four years of the most hilarious rhetoric and no one has ever done more for the meme industry, on the whole. "Big meme" controls political elections but the *normies* haven't figured it out quite yet. A political meme is essentially a political cartoon that you would find in newspapers. To think those little cartoons didn't shape elections in the past is naive. Russia sure did make some dank memes!

Русский бот. *Wink.* The orange man woke up every morning at 5 AM to light Twitter on fire while dropping his morning deuce sitting on his porcelain throne. He literally lived up to the term, "shit poster." Godspeed, sweet Prince.

People got rich riding Trump's coattails, as well. Trump created value, which led to individual freedom. The Babylon Bee understands it. Entire YouTube channels were created in reaction to the democrats. It's why this new "MAGA" just won't go away and it's simply "cause and effect". Greg Gutfeld is now the king of late night comedy television programs due to simply mocking Trump derangement syndrome, while Bill Maher is just holding onto Obama's peener. I could have directed that joke at John Oliver, but 1776 already happened. I couldn't care less about what some "London Silly-Nanny" thinks about America's politics. John Oliver should take a look in the mirror and realize his country is nothing but "East Dakota". And just like the Dakotas here, no one really cares. I find it absolutely disgusting that Bill Maher thinks it is finally time for Millennials and Gen Z to begin taking over the political landscape, after his propaganda machine helped destroy it. He's like a child asking for the adults to come fix his government. *"Muh, gubmit"!* The term "get woke go broke" is very simple to understand. Bill Maher and John Oliver can at least take pride in making the list. "The View" isn't even on the radar! Watching the women of "The View" destroy feminism with institutional feminism has been glorious. I am almost positive that television ratings are based on how many Boomers are passing on to the next life. *Down only.* Every blue moon a libertarian governor comes along and I think, "sure, why not." I chalk it up to collateral damage. It's like throwing pebbles at a statue; it never moves. At least I get to use my veteran status to get out of work to fulfill my patriotic duty and no one dares to question me. Shame the Egoist!

The *real* MAGA understood how funny this all was. The media, both parties, and the large majority of YouTubers still don't understand the *real* MAGA. Micheal Moore was close when he said it was the anarchist last ditch effort to chuck a Molotov cocktail at the White House. He was only wrong in his reasoning. It wasn't to "Make America

Great Again" or bring about some revolution. We always do it for the lulz. It's all we have left and even Cancel Culture is trying to take that away. The current system at the time fell to weaponized meme warfare or "weaponized autism". Imagine, after witnessing all that, how ridiculous this could possibly get? There is a high probability that we could see a Kardasian in the White House some day. If *2024* ends with a Trump re-election along with Sarah Palin as his VP, my funny bone just might break! If you served during the great meme war, what was *your* purpose?

To get back to the point of institutional value. I am simply asking you if the economy sucks because Janet Yellen is a stupid individual, or more so the institutions with which she earned her prestigious degrees, made her stupid. Before Ben Shapiro says yes to both, in all seriousness, an even better question is this: Is she just doing her job serving her constituents? She's an unelected bureaucrat, so she can't be serving yours. I actually wrote this as a joke because Ben graduated from Harvard and Janet graduated from Yale. I just realized Richard Wolff graduated from Yale as well. So should we arrive at the conclusion that we should demolish Yale, in order to pave the way for a more prestigious university such as Ivy Tech? Let's not be too rash, right? Maybe the market is just correcting itself? If that is the case, we live in a capitalist society. The market is regulated through the state. We cannot say it's naturally correcting itself, so someone has to be held responsible. The rich get richer and the world keeps spinning. It's all communism, boys.

The Bitcoin Maximalist should ask themselves this: "Am I wrong in my understanding and my philosophical views in this book?" One can make the argument that I should know my place. I'm not educated well enough to understand the vast complexity of global economics and Bitcoin's purpose/potential. I have no business explaining its value. Nope!! Some of you out there started talking about freedom and it caught my attention. I hold a little Bitcoin, so I'm participating. For me, I have assigned its individual value. Isn't freedom *(anarchy)* fun?!

At the end of the day I trust some Anon living in *Feuchtwangen* running a Bitcoin mining rig powered by a diesel- fueled generator more than my own institutions. They can say that it is an extremist thought, however, but they are thoughts mirrored by the reflection of their own incompetency. In summation: We don't care about institutional legislation defining Bitcoin's freedom. We don't care if you don't understand it. We don't care about institutional value. We don't care if you believe. We're not asking for Bitcoin's freedom. We're simply going to use Bitcoin, the magical internet money!

"Whoever will be free must make himself free. Freedom is no fairy gift to fall into a man's lap. What is freedom? To have the will to be responsible for one's self." - Max Stirner

AGORISM, EGOISM, AND BITISM (SUPER FRENZ)

Wikipedia defines Agorism as a free-market anarchist political philosophy founded by Samuel Edward Konkin III that believes the ultimate goal as bringing about a society in which all "relations between people are voluntary exchanges– a free market. The term comes from the Greek word "agora," referring to an open place for assembly and market in ancient Greek city-states. Agorist theory divides people into two classes: people who make their living through the market, and people who make their living by coercing others (called the "economic class" and "political class", respectively). They support a nonviolent overthrow of the second class by the first, through peaceful black market and grey market activity, known as counter-economics.

Sic Parvis Magna...

The Agorist will pick up quickly on what I'm doing here. In fact, where do you think this all came from? I think the cat is finally out of the bag and it is time everyone understands from where the cryptocurrency ideology really came. Agorism takes a lot of awareness and effort. The ones with talent and skills in regard to the development of markets, blockchain technology, and various cryptocurrencies, may even consider themselves an Agorist.

"An Agonist Primer" was written in 1986 and finally published in 2009. When was Bitcoin created again?? Are you little bunny rabbits putting this together yet? Maybe if we would have had cryptocurrencies back in the 80s, then perhaps we would have moved quickly towards a more open and free-society in regard to markets? Like most great ideas they're often ahead of their time. It's almost humorous in some ways listening to libertarian/anarchists complain about their past governments. Just look at us now boys!! I would love to hear them explain how we're going to pursue our way out of this. I'm pretty sure mass suicide is the only way out of governmental control at this point. (*Don't do mass suicide, it's a joke).*

The Agorist understands perfectly that the pointless attempts of trying to form third-party ideologies to fix any governance system are moot. Samuel Edward Konkin III perfectly illustrates how the libertarian party failed. You can't vote your way out of this. The current two-party system is what it always has been: a civil war. It is simply a distraction, a sideshow, a circus... and I find it hilarious at times. It's unfortunate that I had to drag you into the current culture war, but this is Cryptic Anarchy and this book might send someone down another rabbit hole. Besides, we got to protect the black marke- I mean, the free-market, right??

We see how the state has waged war on all companies, both large and small. Even the individual citizen is being crushed by taxation. This endless onslaught of taxation has absolutely gotten out of hand. Smaller governments are turning on their own communities with absurd regulations and policing for profit. Imagine that! One hundred billion dollars is used per year on policing and another eighty billion is spent on incarceration. But we can't get just one gun toting republican to stop "boot licking". One little raid on Lord Emperor Trump's golden palace, and they all sound like Antifa. *Yawn.*

I feel as though Lady Liberty has now shined her light onto the underground path. Silk Road had too many "speed bumps". *Wink.* Maybe we should try a smaller communal approach? The government was not going to let Bitcoin go unnoticed and Wall Street couldn't stay away from the *gains.* Now, I feel it is time they think we pay. I love how anarchism has branched off in so many ways, personally. I hope Bitism can be an idea traded amongst the tribes, as I don't wish to change anyone's ideologies. I have only observed that all of them consist of currencies and systems of trade.

Some may make the argument Bitism or even Bitcoin is Agorism, and at one point in time I would have agreed. After the years have passed and the community has grown, new currencies have joined the space and new software has been written. Unfortunately we have even begun to write legislation. Things always change with time. Cryptocurrency is too large with too many influencers to have a single ideology. Even the ANCAP reading this is probably thinking, *hmmm, interesting...*

There is literally a "CommieCoin", which you can purchase using "PooCoin"! It must be a combination of several ideologies and it has been around long enough we've seen it in practice. Those that are clever and aware already see a philosophical iceberg forming. I dedicated a good part of my book to explaining DCA, Bitcoin, and the use of Counter-economics freeing more slaves. Not just slaves, or those suffering from slave wages, but those of an institutionalized slave mindset. We can even cause the ruckus and bring some *"razzle dazzle"* to the markets in pure chaotic fashion. Cheers, apes!

Cryptocurrencies are decentralized and transparent. It always goes up and always comes down. It's natural, but I think it might need a different perspective, if you know what I mean. New markets are created every day after all and I don't personally believe the perfect cryptocurrency has been created yet. Honestly I could go much further into all of Samuel's work, but I'd be doing him a better justice by suggesting my readers to enjoy "An Agonist Primer". #SEK3 created the free-market ideology, we supply the currency and the network. By working alongside people in our community we can dent the Fed by casting another rock at it, or perhaps, put another crack in the "ye olde liberty bell". Privacy coins exist already, and we need more "layer ones".

"If you have ever suspected that government, academia, and other entities are attempting to pull the wool over your eyes in order to control your money, your morality, and your life, you find answers and remedies in *(An Agonist Primer)*".

Egoism is a philosophy concerned with the role of the self, or ego, as the motivation and goal of one's own action. Different theories of egoism encompass a range of disparate ideas and can generally be categorized into descriptive or normative forms. That is, they may be interested in either describing that people do act in self-interest or prescribing that they should. Other definitions of egoism may instead emphasize action according to one's will rather than one's self-interest, and furthermore posit that this is a truer sense of egoism.

The New Catholic Encyclopedia states of egoism that it "incorporates in itself certain basic truths: it is natural for man to love himself; he should moreover do so, since each one is ultimately responsible for himself; pleasure, the development of one's potentialities, and the acquisition of power are normally desirable." The moral censure of self-interest is a common subject of critique in egoist philosophy, with such judgments being examined as means of control and the result of power relations. Egoism may also reject that insight into one's internal motivation can arrive extrinsically, such as from psychology or sociology, though, for example, this is not present in the philosophy of Friedrich Nietzsche.

The anarcho-egoist is egoism that can be summed up simply as such: "We are going to do whatever we want, and we don't care how you feel about it!" or "Deal with it". The anarcho-egoist main influence is Max Stirner. There is no arguing his views now that we have seen how governments have grown. Max envisioned and argued for a free-society that works willfully for one another. He believed we were better off trusting our neighbors and small communities. He envisioned that we didn't need third-party interference, i.e. the state, and we were better off left to our own values. Max went as far as to argue against libertarianism, because even then, he knew after two centuries that it would just be called "crony libertarianism". However, due to our unwillingness to listen, Max's ideas have almost become impossible in modern society due to modern warfare. We gave such a rise in power to our governments, and they have created weapons of mass destruction. I know he'd laugh and just call me a spook. I'd laugh back at him and say, "hey, that's why I'm an anarcho-egoist".

Bitists are here to help Max and his Egoist. We want to eliminate third-party inference by eliminating third-party verification during peer-to-peer transactions and freeing individuals from institutional value that is in constant flux due to bureaucracy. There are many advantages to the Egoist involving cryptocurrency. The best examples that come to mind are "rug pulls". A crypto rug pull can be defined as, when a development team abandons a project by selling off all of its liquidity. Or by investing in some scam coin early enough, sell the coin to everyone, and then exit the market leaving them holding the bag. Even the more tame Egoist can find value in cryptocurrencies helping their smaller communities. By applying Agorism and Bitism the Egoist can help reach their communal or individual goals, and they can further their own ideology. My fellow Egoists will understand why this was super fun for me, so I know they get it. I'd also like to suggest that my readers also partake in reading "The Ego and Its Own" by Max Stirner, if you haven't already.

"When the rich wage war, it's the poor who die." -Jean-Paul Sartre

BITISM VS. THE BITCOIN MAXIMALIST

The Bitcoin Maximalist is summed up simply; it's the collective theory that we only need Bitcoin and all other cryptocurrencies are inferior to it.

Boys, we are in the legislative phase of things. Your constitutional rights aren't here to help. We're going to have to get more creative. Make no mistake, I love all my Bitcoin Maximalists and you give me all the energy I need to keep going. You might have just got a little to lose with your overall idea, is all. Are we in the "greater good" phase of things now? Are we buying into "hope"? Micheal Saylor, a.k.a. Saylor Moon, understands Bitcoin and probably explains it better than anyone. My only concern with Micheal is how much are we willing to give up for institutional global adoption. Micheal should have a good understanding that governments don't want peace, and it's one of the many reasons that got us this far in the first place. Bitcoin is money, money funds war. Then does Bitcoin have the potential to fund war? Everything always comes at a price is all I'm saying. Now, before you dismiss everything I'm about to say as only FUD *(fear, uncertainty and doubt).* I'm only going to make you question your institutions while questioning your own ego's purpose.

First, I will start by saying there's been a huge philosophical belief that, "we are all in this together". A Bitist understands situational value is pure value, thus freeing themselves of whatever their ego desires. Property is simply what I control, or what I exercise power over. This doesn't fall in the same realm of collective theories on what property rights are, nor collective theories on value. That's the real *"long con"*, gentlemen. Why do you think people sell?! *Derp.*

Second, you wanted economic freedom through revolutionizing the banking industry. You didn't think it was going to be easy declaring war on the banks, did you? Did anyone watch the Congressional hearing with Charles Hoskinson on CNET? I am very curious what he meant when he said, "It's easier to write the code regulating cryptocurrency after they write the legislation." So is the CEO of Cardano now working for the baddies? Weird, right? Charles Hoskinson is the Bill Gates of Web3. I know a squealer when I see one. What's next? CoinTracker 2.0? They are many years ahead of us on tracking and now they're talking about legislation. Where do you see this going? What will become of the masses?

The third argument is really "What is money?" In the poorest of countries, people use Pokemon cards as currencies. How the hell does everyone in these third-world countries have i-Phones and the internet, yet use such a primitive way to trade? Sounds pretty ridiculous right? They can now create their own cryptocurrencies and create a more modern way to trade. It also gives them the ability to access a free-market and offers them the security that comes with using blockchain technology. Let them free themselves. Let them make their own coins and markets. Do not say they have to use Bitcoin. That is absolutely ridiculous. The value is in the code. We use whatever cryptocurrency is necessary to meet our own personal or small communal needs. We don't want just one coin. If that truly is the Maximalist ideology then you might as well call it what it really is, "Marxist Coin"! Chaos is fair and chaos keeps us further from the center. This is the Bitist way. Ask yourself what layer one is. Before answering, I want you to close your eyes, think really hard, and see where your imagination leads you into the future. Then, please, keep it to yourself.

My fourth and final argument is... Well boys, you won.

Bitcoin is better than gold and there's no getting around it. It's the best money on earth. But now that it's better than gold and worthy of a title asset, is it no longer a currency? Of course, it's still a currency, but what I'm getting at is the taxes. The power is out of our hands now. The government can simply raise capital gains tax and write legislation taxing peer-to-peer transactions. They can kill the network and limit its capabilities by simply taxing us. Or you can at least admit it will have costly effects. The government pointed a gun at Bitcoin. What will you do? Roll over as they tax you to death? I know at the end of the day we are not all going to agree on how much Bitcoin is taxed, thus demonstrating, yet again, a failed democracy. Taxation is theft! I know it and you know it. It is what got us here in the first place. So roll the dice, Fed boy. Last time this country had a tax revolt, things got hell of a lot more interesting.

To quote Alex Jones, "I'm going to be honest, I'm *kind* of retarded".

Dogecoin is my back up plan, gentlemen. Do it for the lulz! We might as well be one of the few to light the match and get this fire started. Resistance is futile at this point. It is a difficult job for institutions to sell dog money as a global currency and its been called the people's money for a reason. Bitcoin is becoming a victim of its own success. We are going to see this through, and we don't care which coin gets used to do it. We can make this as ridiculous as the government wants us to make it. It's simply this; if the institutions are going to tax us to death using Bitcoin and cryptocurrencies, I would rather they do it in dog money. At the end of the day if replacing our forefathers with a dog meme serves their best interest then they made their choice. Maybe if we are lucky enough, we can get a dog statue beside Dick Cheney's statue. I feel that we understand Bitcoin's potential. What's Dogecoin's potential? *"Mount Dogemore"?* They made a mockery of our institutions first. If society chooses to file their taxes, let it be a constant reminder of the institutions' failure. There are many holes to Fed boy, "Bertrand Russell was a psyop"!

Cryptocurrency is a psyop??

After the cyber hornets are done dragging me online for giving Bitcoin a misconception or bad definition, they can look into the mirror and make the argument, "if you stick your peener in a hornets' nest, you'll probably get stung." Diogenes might say, "there's not enough honey in this nest". Hornets don't make honey, and we need that sweetness. My logic is undeniable. The only suitable reaction to this book is Billy Markus writing Doge-ism Cryptic Memes. A philosophy based primarily from Diogenes, the All-father himself. This isn't an attempt to discourage all my Bitcoin

Maximalists. I'm just curious if you even know what you're doing at this point? A Bitist understands, unlike a Bitcoin Maximalist, the importance and pleasure it is to have Dogecoin. Shame the Egoist and all his joys!

For as much shit as they talked about Dogecoin being a stupid meme coin, Billy accidentally gave them their only way to protest. *Nice.*

"It's not about the money, it's about sending a message." -The Joker

I know everyone wanted to hear this grand Utopian conclusion, but I'll leave that for the Bitcoin Maximalist. The Bitcoin Maximalist if they wish to maintain their idea, they will have a difficult time with mass adoption. If the idea is to now teach the masses on how to avoid taxes, in theory if possible, then we wouldn't need Bitcoin to begin with. They can also always ban companies from using cryptocurrency or even ban exchanges in some countries. I wish them the best but they shouldn't underestimate DeFi capabilities. Ethereum isn't a threat to Bitcoin, but it is definitely useful and the majority of financial applications are built on Ethereum. I hold Vitalik Buterin the creator of Ethereum in high regard, because of his brilliance and philosophical views involving cryptocurrency. I do not particularly care for the idea of governance tokens, but some human influence should matter in future market applications. After all, we are building it for ourselves. To think Bitcoin isn't slowly becoming a governance coin is a little naive. We are witnessing this becoming a game of *Commies Vs. Cowboys*. I'll ask the Maximalist again, what is layer one? Please remember to keep it to yourself.

The Maximalists seem to have a lot of confidence and, in all fairness, I will admit they have cold storage and exchanges all over the world to avoid tyrannical governments. However, I find the Maximalist desperate at times, and they seem to cling to whomever is pumping Bitcoin. They're still looking for the tip of their spear instead of just relying on the technology. The Maximalist will tell you everything is going to plan and that they are inevitable. The individual anarchist will tell you that they have heard this rhetoric a million times. Ideologies that pose any threat to the already existing hierarchy will always be manipulated and led astray. Personally, I'm debating myself whether George Orwell or Aldous Huxley got it right.

I've read enough manifestos, so I won't bother trying to over complicate it, wasting mine and everyone's time. It's nothing but speculation, and the ones before me get it wrong all the time. Should this book hold merit as I am a time traveler, and in the year *2054* McDonald's created WWIV by discontinuing the McRib, causing mass global famine? *Derp.* Never underestimate the willingness of conformity and behaviorism should always be taken into account when discussing your arguments in regard to changing or predicting the future. In every single manifesto, they all have a currency and systems of trade. The key is still in small communal needs. Your actions will define what Bitcoin is to you and its future, nothing more.

Yawn Are we waking up yet?

This next message is to those in control of various institutions: Congratulations on failing to maintain the institution's value! America's greatness through institutional eyes can only be measured by how many unborn children we kill or by how many McDonald's we have per square mile. Watching you fighting against being replaced by software, under the false pretext that our democracy is at stake, has brought us much joy. Shame the Egoist!

If you want to be stupid, we can be really stupid. We can make this as ridiculous as the institutions want to make it. We'll play their game. Show us your butt-hole!! Representative Brad Sherman gets it!! Mongoose coin to the moon!! *"The future is now, old man"*...

Welcome to decentralized monetary democracy, or magical internet money!

"Anarchism is the great liberator of man from the phantoms that have him captive; it is the arbiter and pacifier of the two forces for individual and social harmony." -Emma Goldman

WHAT'S MONEY LITTLE BUNNY

This book would be nothing without some poetry and riddles. As we sail forward into uncharted waters and through bear markets, it is important to maintain our spirits. Let those that "didn't make it" be remembered through our melody. *R.I.P. Luna..*

What's money??

Man's desire..

Hive is to honey..

What's money little bunny??

Thought man, first conspired..

What's money??

Only man's desire..

It's been a long journey down the rabbit hole, so rest here weary traveler. I got just the thing to lift your spirits. I know you want to sing sea shanties with the boys, so let's go!!

Oh I grab anchor and wait for the boys, Our lulz boat is filling up with more haxxor toys.
As we cast sail and wait for fair winds, We look to the ones by our side as true frenz.
The storm blows wild and the seas open wide, We will not dwell on what's been left behind.
Those thrown from our boat as it glides ever high, We will remember you as you were so don't cry.
As we sail forward into untold surprises, Wherever we end up there are new sunrises.
Hurry now boys and hoist our black flag, Fair lands lie ahead and there's plenty to snag.
We are the boys of these fair lands, So why won't you join us and welcome our stand, Hurry now lad and come take my hand... WAGMI! (we all gonna make it)

*Side note: The shanty is more enjoyable sung to the melody of "Bones in the Ocean" by The Longest Johns.

Now that we sang Cerberus to sleep, we may finally enter our final chapter. Just like the previous chapters, we're going to stay savage. No turning back now little bunny. Let's finally see what lies at the end of the rabbit hole.

"Anarchism, to me, means not only the denial of authority, not only a new economy, but a revision of the principles of morality. It means the development of the individual as well as the assertion of the individual. It means self-responsibility, and not leader worship" -Voltaire de Cleyre

DIOGENES THE ALL-FATHER

The anarchist is mocked, shamed, outcast, and ridiculed. The institutions murder, yet they call us volatile. Diogenes was the first true stoic. He was known as The Dog. He has always been the man holding the lantern shining light onto man's hypocrisies and moral dilemmas. Do not pity the homeless; become envious. We can all just opt-out and play homeless tag in the parks. We can live our best lives as beggars. It is the institutions that are so desperate to maintain their relevance! After witnessing the way some of you trade cryptocurrency you might some day need a stoic mindset. *Wink.*

The majority of stoic philosophers throughout history have tried to bury and forget Diogenes because of his animalistic behavior and absurd ideologies that he would display willfully in public. This is our bukkake at the cyber-agora of assertiveness, so you better hide more sensitive eyes, as this is the dance of market exorcism. Some refer to Diogenes as "the cynic", but that was the stoic's attempt to disregard his teachings and distance themselves from Diogenes. Even though cynicism is found in his teachings it is part of the trinity for stoics to practice. No one likes an armchair therapist and Diogenes displayed stoicism everyday in life. Stoics of the past tried to create a more sensible practice to living in order to remain their relevance in the eyes of the public. You can compare this to most religions whose past has been rewritten time after time. Like words on the computer screen they have become more meaningless.

Socrates was right!! Plato underestimated the importance of human dialogue or face to face interaction. Human intimacy begins with conversation, that is the gateway to spiritual consultation. Only in our relationship with others are we spiritually whole. Artificial human intimacy has left humanity drained of its compassion, as words lost their way leaving their master's expressions. Philosophy dies with every text as artificial hearts melt compressed sand, as it simmers thoughts in empty theaters. It is in that thought; that has made me question whether Plato was correct in saying, "democracy is good". Look at how meaningless democracy has become. It sounds absolutely ridiculous to say democracy is bad, but even more so, to say that it works. Those that disagree should look me in the eye. Only through someone's eyes can we see their soul. Diogenes was wise enough to never put someone on the pedestal to begin with. Collectively there is no going back, but I know what Diogenes would do. He would deface the currency, lulz, so do!! Sometimes boys you just got to start "pressing pickle". *Dicks out for Harambe!* Diogenes' statue was erected in Sinop, Turkey, where he was born. In his honor, it reads, "Even bronze grows old with time, but your fame, Diogenes not all Eternity shall take away. For you alone did point out to mortals the lessons of self-sufficiency and the path for the best and easiest life."

*Side note: Another honorable mention amongst philosophers is, Georg Wilhelm Friedrich Hegel. Hopefully once this book is decrypted, Hegel's petri dish will finally be exposed. Hegel was in fact more or less the Anti-Christ! *(If you know, you know...)*

This book was my best effort to embrace Diogenes' teachings and what he might say about the current culture war and the institutions of today. He would find them worthless and a waste of his precious time. Diogenes was too self-sufficient to listen or need collective ideologies of institutional governance. There is probably a good reason Diogenes out lived both the philosophers, and the emperors of his time. It could have been divinity or chaos magic, but he was definitely meant to be remembered. If you take a good look into Diogenes' life and you are not left amazed and somewhat puzzled. Well, my friend, you're a more interesting person than I. Was Diogenes the first "internet troll"? *Behold! I've brought you Plato's interwebz!*

Don't be the problem, be the entire problem. We took the most stoic approach and yawned at the boredom of current ideologies and their repetitive talking points. As if to say, get out of our sunlight. I am a Millennial, after all, so I find it impossible to believe or acknowledge the never-ending, meaningless banter older generations have displayed thus far. Even the mind-numbing rants I've concocted are a consequence of the individual who has stared at the orb too long, as if we are all moths to the light. We live a web of lies and I know subconsciously you'll understand.

I overthink therefore I over am??

A more positive outtake could be that this is the consequence of leaving your knife on the sharpening stone too long. Cuts like a razor, but still feels flimsy. That could be the best way to describe most anarchist. By that, I mean we can cut through the moral corruption like butter but our ideas are scary and seem uncertain to institutionalized individuals. We don't want too much freedom, right?!

I tried to keep it playful and childish because we're only joking around and speculating. This book is a meme, so have fun with it. Younger generations meme everything because it's all just a joke anyways. Friedrich Nietzsche created his own style of writing, and I thought, meme lives matter. I don't want to be thought of as a pessimist and I have been very critical of a lot of institutions. Personally, I feel people that get labeled as pessimist are from those that are pulled into the future without giving any historical thought.

There is only one institution that, throughout my life, has truly stood out. The fire department, truly is the beacon of humanity. Their duty is that of self-sacrifice. I've personally watched a fireman run into a burning building to save a dog. Nothing about that is logical. Their bravery and willingness to lay down their own individual value in a moment's notice goes unmatched against all institutions. I'm grateful to have them. They lead the way, and this is the way.

I wanted to keep this book short, yet limitless. Teach without leading. I left a lot of room for open-mindedness, because it's not my idea to explain. If the theory of "God Money" is to exist, then let it restore your free will. You have suffered enough rule of man and it's time to make your own. This book is for the reader to research and come to their own conclusions. I get so tired of people writing things as "facts" when we're dealing with speculation. The majority of time while I'm reading, I find the author continuously stroking their own ego in the attempt to gain popularity. I feel I did an excellent job displaying that for my own personal pleasure. Again, teach without leading. If you hand someone the sword you are left weaponless so choose wisely. We need no leaders as we only need individuals that are uniquely qualified from our own individual perspective to influence us. Find the ones you can relate with most and bring them closer. New coins, markets, and blockchains are created every day due to free thought. I didn't want to limit people's evolution to just one coin or ideology with fancy terminology or "science". I find it insulting that venture capitalist, mainstream media, and the vast majority of institutions believe we can't see or think for ourselves. In their defense, I will say, there are a lot of what they refer to as "useful idiots".

There are no conclusions to this book involving cryptocurrencies and just like cryptocurrency, we are in constant motion. Hopefully this book gave you an idea while entering this "new" market-cycle. We created the trinity for the greatest rug pull in history. You just need to create your own path. Now go find freedom, little bunny.

A Bitist mindset is simple. Freedom can be best described as an individual emotion derived from the individual's current environment. In other words, it's all perspective. Freedom can not be defined using collective theory and politicians have proven that. Self-liberation begins with knowing your own value.

The value of Bitcoin and other cryptocurrencies lies within the code and community, not in its current market capitalization nor institutional collective theories on value. Cryptocurrency is money in motion that has lifted the veil on how the scales are balanced. Cryptocurrency is merely a solution to another growing problem, because everything moves in an endless upgraded cycle. Once a cycle becomes corrupted, we maintain the Bitist mindset and move forward with new inventive ideas, criticizing by creating.

We value individual self-interest before all others, as we know we are all acting in our own best interests. We create value from our individual perspective which leads to harmony instead of conformist oppression. Philosophy can be situational as well, and it's all speculation. It's probably why Diogenes found it a waste of time. Chaotic good characters were individualist like Diogenes, who took actions of kindness and altruism. In other words, it's called chaotic good, not chaotic nice. Deface the currency, literally and culturally.

Protect your own ideas, not someone else's idea, "do stuff". This is the way.

Diogenes' honor, I would like to write, "Dogecoin to the moon!"

WE ARE <u>D</u>YNAMIC, WE ARE <u>C</u>HAOS, WE ARE <u>A</u>UTONOMOUS

(This is philosophically financial advice)

(nice)

Printed in the United States
by Baker & Taylor Publisher Services